Small Community Leader Guide

for

WHY CATHOLIC?

JOURNEY THROUGH THE CATECHISM

A Formation Resource

RENEW
INTERNATIONAL

NIHIL OBSTAT
Reverend Lawrence E. Frizzell, D.Phil.
Censor Librorum

IMPRIMATUR
Most Reverend John J. Myers, D.D., J.C.D.
Archbishop of Newark

Illustrator Angela Albertazzi
Graphic Design by Linda L. Eberly

ISBN 1-930978-27-8

Published by RENEW International
1232 George Street
Plainfield, NJ 07062-1717
Phone 908-769-5400
E-mail whycatholic?@renewintl.org
www.whycatholic.org
www.renewintl.org

Printed and bound in the United States of America

TABLE OF CONTENTS

The richness of our Catholic faith is always unfolding. Whether our formal education was for a few years or many, adults need to continue to unfold the mysteries of our faith. For that reason, RENEW International has taken the four parts of the *Catechism of the Catholic Church* and has developed a four-book series, *Why Catholic? Journey through the Catechism*.

Small Community Leader Guide for Why Catholic? is designed to assist small community leaders to prepare for the *Why Catholic?* process. Leaders are encouraged to attend the *Why Catholic?* Leader Formation in their parish or diocese. Where this is not possible, a staff person or lay leader can use this formation resource to gather leaders to prepare them for their crucial role in leading a *Why Catholic?* small community.

As a small community leader, you will be helping those in a small community to read, pray over, and treasure the rich resources of the *Catechism of the Catholic Church* by using the books in the *Why Catholic?* Series. *Why Catholic?* invites participants to a mature faith by nourishing and strengthening them in their calling and identity as Catholic Christians. By using these materials, we hope participants will study the *Catechism of the Catholic Church* in greater depth, internalize its teachings, share faith in Jesus Christ, and let their faith illuminate every aspect of their lives.

The four books will also be a way for people to uncover their own story, their own journey about being

Catholic. Solidly based on the content of the *Catechism of the Catholic Church*, the series includes

- ❒ *The Profession of Faith: What We Believe*
- ❒ *The Celebration of the Christian Mystery: Sacraments*
- ❒ *Life in Christ: Walking with God*
- ❒ *Christian Prayer: Deepening My Experience of God*

You will notice the section entitled "Preparation for *Why Catholic?* Themes" is divided into four subsections corresponding to the four *Why Catholic?* books. In each subsection there is a schema, information on adult faith formation, and session highlights. You may want to refer to the session highlights while preparing for your meeting.

As Christians we are called to be a faith community, a community in which people can come to know one another and share their faith and life—thus unleashing the mighty power of the Spirit.

RENEW is looking to reinforce this vision. As part of this process, you will provide leadership to a unique small community called by God to be God's presence in the world. What a great gift you have been offered!

Spiritual Preparation

"We will share with them the living word of God, which can touch their hearts and minds... [w]e will trust the capacity of prayer and sacrament to open their eyes to the presence and love of Christ."

(*Our Hearts Were Burning Within Us [OHWB]*, USCCB, 9)

Praying *A Disciple's Prayer* and reflecting on the Emmaus story are simple ways to prepare yourself spiritually before the small community meeting.

A DISCIPLE'S PRAYER

Loving God and Father,
help us to be people of prayer,
committed to the person and message of Jesus your Son.

Help us to grasp the integrity and beauty
of the truths of our faith and
the transforming power of your grace.

Nourish and strengthen us as people of faith,
disciples of Jesus, committed to the mission of the Church
and eager to share the gospel without restraint.

Let our hearts burn within us
as we catch glimpses of your heart in Jesus,
for through him, we know your loving plan for us.

We ask this through Jesus the Christ who lives
with you and the Holy Spirit
in one loving Trinity. Amen

(Based on *Our Hearts Were Burning Within Us* by U.S. Catholic Bishops.)

In preparation for leading a *Why Catholic?* small community, pray *A Disciple's Prayer* and spend some time in silent reflection on your role as facilitator.

EMMAUS REFLECTION

You may also choose to prepare for leading a *Why Catholic?* small community by reading the Emmaus story (Luke 24:13-32). What better way to reflect on leadership than to look to the example of God who walked among us? Jesus walked with people, asked questions, listened attentively to their stories, touched their hearts and minds by sharing with them the living Word of God. He spoke through word and sacrament and invited them to live and share the Good News. Jesus is a model teacher—a servant leader, first among equals, companion on the journey. To be a leader, you do not have to be a theologian, rather, simply a companion on the journey.

Read the Emmaus story slowly to yourself. After a few minutes of silence, read the story again. Ask yourself the following questions:

- From the perspective of being a leader, what word or phrase from this story has meaning for me?
- What are some specific ways I can be a servant leader to my small community?

ADULT LEARNING IN SMALL COMMUNITIES

"Small communities are powerful vehicles for adult faith formation providing opportunities for learning, prayer, mutual support, and the shared experience of Christian living and service to Church and society."

(*OHWB*, USCCB, 106)

"Adults do not grow in faith primarily by learning concepts, but by sharing the life of the Christian community" (*OHWB*, USCCB, 83). "Small communities can be an effective way in which to deepen our spirituality." This section highlights the structure of small Christian communities and the role of the Small Community Leader.

WHAT IS A SMALL CHRISTIAN COMMUNITY?

A small Christian community is a face-to-face gathering of six to twelve people who invest time with one another for the common purpose of applying gospel values to every aspect of their lives. In addition, small communities that gather to use *Why Catholic?* focus on the rich resources of the truths and beliefs of our Catholic faith.These communities come together once a week or every other week in people's homes for about 1½ hours in order to

- ❒ read and reflect on the Scriptures and Church teachings
- ❒ pray together
- ❒ share each other's lives and faith
- ❒ respond in action

For a group to become a small Christian community, these five key elements need to be present.

PRAYER

The element of prayer emphasizes the centrality of God's active presence in each small Christian community member's life and in the life of the community itself.

SHARING

Members talk freely about God and about life experiences, reflecting on these in light of Scripture and Tradition.

LEARNING

Because small Christian communities are part of the wider Church they are called to an ever fuller knowledge and understanding of the gospel, of the Catholic Church and its teaching on faith and morals, and of the relationship of that teaching to the circumstances and issues of their members' lives.

MUTUAL SUPPORT

In a society in which gospel values are all too frequently ridiculed and rejected, the believer needs a community that is supportive of these values. The small Christian community encourages fidelity to the gospel and also challenges itself and its members to a more profound and authentic commitment to Christian living.

MISSION

Authentic Christian communities are, like Jesus, committed to a life of loving mission or service. As a group and through its individual members, the community will work for compassion, justice, reconciliation, and peace within the group, in the family, in the workplace, in the neighborhood, and within the wider society.

FOCUS AREAS FOR SMALL COMMUNITY LEADERS

YOUR ROLE

The small community leader is a facilitator of learning, not the teacher.The following three points stress the basic principles of adult learning:

Adult learning

- ❒ is participative
- ❒ allows people to speak from their own experience
- ❒ involves learning from one another as people share wisdom, knowledge, and experiences

As a small community leader, you will want to focus on the following six areas to ensure the ongoing spiritual growth of the individual members of your small community as well as the small community itself.

1. MENTORING THE COMMUNITY

As the leader of your small community, you are responsible for guiding and encouraging the small community in a pastoral way.

- ❒ Welcome, provide hospitality, and be attentive to the needs of the individuals and the community. Keep in touch with them between meetings, especially when someone misses a meeting.
- ❒ An important part of your task will also be to encourage each person in the community to be caring to one another.

2. FACILITATING ADULT FAITH FORMATION

In the U.S. Bishops' document on adult faith formation, *Our Hearts Were Burning Within Us: A Pastoral Plan for Adult Faith Formation in the United States*, it says that knowledge of faith comes through exploring "the Scriptures so that adults may be hearers and doers of the word" (91). Your overall responsibility with regard to the content of *Why Catholic?* is to help people become more familiar with both the Word of God and the *Catechism of the Catholic Church* and to lead people to "a living, explicit, and fruitful confession of faith" (*General Directory for Catechesis* 82).

- ❐ Make sure that all members have a Bible.
- ❐ Go through the Bible and point out how to read it (i.e., books, chapters, verses) (especially if this is a new experience for some members of the community.)
- ❐ Encourage them to purchase or borrow a *Catechism of the Catholic Church* for their own reference.
- ❐ Point out the four parts of the *Catechism of the Catholic Church* and how to locate information through paragraph numbers.

3. GIVING NEW LIFE TO PRAYER

Any person whose life is truly centered in God engages in conversation with God. This open and sincere conversation is called prayer. Through this conversation with God, we see more clearly our path in life. We pray prayers of blessing and adoration, petition, thanksgiving, and praise. Prayer is not only a matter of words. We can pray in silence and by meditating on the words of Scripture. We can also contemplate the goodness of God.

- ❒ Deepen your own personal prayer life and set the stage for prayer within the community.
- ❒ Begin and end each meeting with prayer.
- ❒ Use various forms of prayer and invite others to lead the prayer in the community. (See *Small Christian Communities: A Vision of Hope for the 21st Century* Revised and Expanded, 2003, Chapter 14.)
- ❒ Help the community to grow in prayer by taking time for silence and spontaneous prayers of love and gratitude.
- ❒ Invite each member to grow in his or her own personal prayer life.

4. ATTENDING TO GROUP DYNAMICS

The small community leader is responsible for the group dynamics. Some examples include

Listening	Listen to each person with total attentiveness and encourage others to do the same.
Paraphrasing	Check to see if you understood the other person's comments by saying, in your own words, what you thought was said.
Supporting	Affirm and support others in what they share and the ways they are trying to live their faith.
Clarifying	If there is a misunderstanding, try to clarify the situation by restating what people are saying.
Focusing	If the group is straying from the topic, ask a pertinent question to return people to the theme or the Scripture.
Directing	When appropriate, invite the quieter person to share, and remind the person who speaks often to give others an opportunity to share.

5. FOSTERING GOOD LEADERSHIP SKILLS

As a small community leader, be faithful to the following leadership skills:

- ❐ Be sensitive to the needs of everyone. Reach out—both at the meeting and between meetings to those who may be hurting.
- ❐ Challenge the community to growth. Gently, but firmly, encourage the community to live gospel values.
- ❐ Set the stage for growth in faith. Pay attention to all the details for a reflective, prayerful, open, accepting climate.
- ❐ Be humble. Be a servant leader, not someone who controls.
- ❐ Be in relationship with the larger Church. You are a liaison between your small community and the parish community.
- ❐ Forgive. Always be open to forgive and be forgiven.
- ❐ Celebrate. Find ways to celebrate both within the small community meetings and outside meetings by planning Christmas parties, summer picnics, outreach to the community, etc. Include families.

6. MOVING THE COMMUNITY TO GOSPEL ACTION

One of the most challenging aspects of small communities is reaching out to the broader world and carrying the mission of Jesus into all aspects of life. Becoming "cozy" support groups is not enough.

- ❒ Make sure that you prepare well each week for the "Living the Good News" component of the meeting.
- ❒ Gather service ideas from the parish, diocese, neighborhood, town, or city.
- ❒ Begin each session by inviting people to share how they lived the Good News during the previous week. If it is difficult for people to do this, be sure to talk about your own experience as an example.

The Church's pastoral ministry exists to sustain the work of the Gospel. One way it does this is by nourishing and strengthening lay men and women in their calling and identity as people of fatih, as contributors to the life and work of the Church, and as disciples whose mission is to the world. To grow in discipleship throughout life, all believers need and are called to build vibrant parish and diocesan communities of faith and service.

Our Hearts Were Burning Within Us 3

Small Community Leader Skills

"In their various forms [small] groups provide genuine support to people in living their faith in daily life."

(*OHWB*, USCCB, 105)

"The ministry of leadership in small communities is a very specific service that lay persons can render" (*Small Christian Communities: A Vision of Hope for the 21st Century*, Revised and Expanded, 2003, p. 173). Small community leaders take on a significant role as they share in the pastoral care of their small communities. This section highlights aspects of being a good leader and facilitator so that the group will have a good and faith-filled experience.

YOUR RESPONSIBILITIES AS A SMALL COMMUNITY LEADER

BEFORE THE SMALL COMMUNITY MEETING

- ❒ Pray for each member of your small community.
- ❒ Visit each member personally before the first gathering in order to introduce yourself and give each one the necessary materials.
- ❒ Inform each member of the location for the gathering as well as the day and time.
- ❒ Prepare well by reviewing the weekly process, the theme of the session, the Scripture texts, the appropriate section of the *Catechism*, and reflection questions.
- ❒ Prepare possible "Living the Good News" responses, that is, action responses for yourself and your small community.
- ❒ Create a prayerful environment for the gathering, e.g., flowers or a plant, a circle of chairs, lighting, an open Bible, a *Catechism*, a candle, etc.

DURING THE SMALL COMMUNITY MEETING

- ❒ Make each and every member feel welcomed and accepted, especially when members begin to share their stories.
- ❒ Maintain a prayerful environment and promote participation by seeing that each person is given the opportunity to share.
- ❒ **Remember that your role is facilitator, not teacher.** Hold the community to the meeting agenda without assuming the role of "teacher." When doctrinal questions surface, refer them to the pastor or a pastoral staff member. (This also gives the pastor the opportunity to recognize general interest in topics that could be important to the whole parish.)
- ❒ The small communities are not intended to be problem solving. A small community is an inappropriate setting to deal with emotionally-laden issues of a personal nature. The leader is clearly not to enter the realm of treating people with their emotional, in-depth feelings such as depression, anxiety, and intense anger. When someone moves in this direction, beyond faith sharing, the leader should bring the community back to faith sharing. With the help of the pastor and/or the pastoral staff, the person should be advised to seek the assistance of professional counseling.

- ❒ Draw out reticent participants in a non-threatening, gentle, and understanding manner. Remember, each person is encouraged to share at the level he or she is most comfortable.
- ❒ Direct the person who is overbearing or too talkative, explaining the need to allow others to share.
- ❒ Keep the focus on the content of the session. When the conversation strays to another topic, refocus the group.
- ❒ Share tasks such as timekeeping, reading, leading prayer, providing light refreshments after the meeting, etc.
- ❒ Ensure confidentiality.
- ❒ Assist participants in discovering their story by recommending they keep a journal. At the conclusion of each session, remind them to spend some time journaling key beliefs of the Catholic Church and their personal insights.

AFTER THE SMALL COMMUNITY MEETING

- ❐ Review your own efforts with honesty and compassion.
- ❐ Follow up on any questions that may have surfaced during the meeting.
- ❐ Continue praying for each member of your community and ask the Holy Spirit to guide the community.
- ❐ Communicate with those members who signed up but did not attend, and continue to invite them to come.

AFTER THE GROUP CONCLUDES EACH BOOK OF WHY CATHOLIC?

- ❐ Distribute evaluation forms. (See Handouts 9a-9d in *How to Use* Why Catholic? *in Your Parish*.) Allow time for members to complete them. After you and the *Why Catholic?* Coordinator read them, please return them to RENEW International.

Further resources for your small community. There are four books in the *Why Catholic?* Series. Choose another one to continue your faith journey together. These and other resources are available from RENEW International. (See p. 74 for ordering information.)

POINTS TO PONDER

Time	Flexibility is essential. Try to work within the 1½ hour schedule. People's time is important. However, the group may agree to meet for a two-hour period for some of the longer sessions or may choose to finish the rest of the session at another time.
Song	Some small communities love to sing. Choose songs that are appropriate and that you can readily find. While suggestions are given, they serve merely as suggestions.
Questions	The questions are designed to encourage faith sharing, not to be answered rigidly. The final question usually encourages participants to put their faith into action.
Silence	There is a great deal of material in each of the sessions. It may be appropriate to read "Exploring the *Catechism*" silently some of the time. Allow time for people to reflect.

Remember that as the leader you are not the "answer person" or the teacher. Share leadership responsibilities such as prayer, hospitality, etc.

Any small community needs to be open to new people. When we welcome others, we are being true followers of Jesus.

HELPFUL HINTS FOR SMALL COMMUNITY LEADERS

IF THIS HAPPENS	LEADER MIGHT RESPOND
Interrupting, jumping in	"Maybe we could stop for a moment to be sure we are listening to each other."
Two people talking at once	"We seem to have two conversations going on here; maybe we could hear from X first and then Y."
No response to questions	"Perhaps the question is difficult to respond to; let's reword it, (or ask another question related to it)."
Member remains silent	Gently invite participation, reaffirm the right to silence. Get to know the person before and after the meeting. Say, "___ , you have been listening intently. Is there anything you'd like to add?"
Repetition of the same idea	Summarize the person's main points and go on. Say: "That's helpful. Maybe we could hear now from someone else."

Wandering from the topic	"To bring ourselves back to the purpose of our sharing, it appears the basic question here is...."
One member dominates the session	Remind the member that each person needs to have the opportunity to share before we hear from the same person again. Say, "What you are saying is helpful, but maybe we could hear from someone else." Remind the group of the guidelines written in the front of the booklet.
A member is very angry	Listen carefully and acknowledge the person's need to express his or her anger. The leader doesn't have to take the anger away or fix it.
A member begins to cry	Comfort any way you are able. Offer the option to be silent for a few minutes. Acknowledge the person and how he or she is feeling.
If a person disagrees with a doctrine or teaching of the Church	Thank the person for his or her input. Say "I encourage you to speak with the pastor or pastoral staff person about this matter. For now, could we look at the questions and come back to the focus of the session."

BRIDGES TO EFFECTIVE LISTENING

Listen by using my whole body. Let my body language show that I am listening (open body stance, direct eye contact, lean forward slightly).

Listen by being truly present to the speaker and giving undivided attention (not doing something else at the same time I am supposedly listening).

Listen by acknowledging the speaker's feelings. ("I can hear that you have a lot of feelings around this topic," "You sound very sad.") Don't minimize, sermonize, or negate.

Listen by observing. The words the speaker says are only part of the story. Be mindful of the facial expressions, tone of voice, and body language in order to better interpret what you are hearing. Do the words match the body language? If not, some clarifying is in order.

Listen by putting aside my own needs. I need to allow the person to speak and not protect my comfort by changing the subject or making a joke to relieve tension. I can acknowledge that I don't have a similar experience so I don't really know how the speaker feels but I want to listen anyway.

Listen by keeping focused on the speaker and speaker's experience, without planning my response or anticipating what the speaker will say before it is said.

Listen by not problem solving, giving unasked for and unwanted advice, and remembering that the focus is to listen and not to "fix it."

Listen by allowing the speaker's point of view, by giving up my need to be right, and by not arguing my own point.

Listen by paraphrasing and asking clarifying questions so the speaker knows that I heard and understood what was said.

BARRIERS TO EFFECTIVE LISTENING

Minimizing	downplaying someone's opinion: "It could be worse" or "It will get better."
Sermonizing	saying: "It's God's will." "You must have faith."
Selecting	choosing what is comfortable to listen to or what fits your experience.
Negating	denying the other person his or her feelings. "You shouldn't feel that way…."
Planning	thinking of a response or solution and not really hearing.
Anticipating	determining what will be said before it happens.
Topping	focusing on your own story: "My story's better than your story."
Arguing	debating to prove a point of view.
Pacifying	agreeing in order to be liked or accepted: "Of course," "I know what you mean," "How wonderful!," Really?," "Uh huh...uh huh," or "Great!"

Redirecting	changing the subject or "lightening up" an uncomfortable atmosphere through humor.
Justifying	maintaining a strong need to be right.
Shutting Out	interrupting or cutting off another person; paying no attention to the previous comment.

GUIDELINES FOR WELCOMING PRIESTS TO SMALL COMMUNITIES

❒ Invite your parish priest(s) to visit and participate in your small community.

❒ Extend a warm welcome.

❒ Be understanding of his calendar and other responsibilities.

❒ Don't make the priest the "Answer Man" at the meeting. Allow him to participate in the same relaxed manner as others in the group.

❒ As with any participant, an atmosphere of love and support are important. This is meant to be a positive experience.

❒ Be reasonable in your expectations of your priest's response. Don't be judgmental if your priest is unable to accept your invitation.

HOW TO USE THE FAITH-SHARING BOOK

This book helps communities to reflect on the Scriptures and the *Catechism of the Catholic Church*. It is most helpful if some members of the group or the group as a whole have the Scriptures and a copy of the *Catechism of the Catholic Church (CCC)* at their meeting. Encourage participants to keep a journal as part of their faith-sharing experience. Journaling can be an important way for them to note key beliefs and personal insights.

The following is helpful in understanding how to use *Why Catholic?*

- ❒ Some sentences are direct quotes from the *Catechism*. The direct quotes are in bold print.
- ❒ Some of the material is summarized and paraphrased; whether directly quoted or paraphrased, material from the *Catechism* is identified by the paragraph number (not page number) from the *Catechism* in bold and in parentheses, that is **(000)**.
- ❒ Prayer must always be at the heart of our Christian gatherings. The term **Lifting Our Hearts** is used to indicate prayer.
- ❒ Each week an action response is recommended. This response, termed **Living the Good News**, allows the participant to bring the reflection into his or her daily life.

❒ The **Looking Ahead** section allows both leaders and participants the opportunity to prepare for the next session. It is suggested that you prayerfully read and study the recommended material.

THE WHY CATHOLIC? PROCESS

The *Why Catholic?* process is usually scheduled for 1½ hours. The process is as follows:

Introductions (when the group is new or when someone joins the group)

10 min.	Lifting Our Hearts
5 min.	Living the Good News from previous sharing session
10 min.	Exploring the *Catechism*
15 min.	Scripture Passage and Sharing Question
10 min.	Continued Exploring the *Catechism*
25 min.	Sharing Our Faith
5 min.	Living the Good News
10 min.	Lifting Our Hearts

Preparation for Why Catholic? Themes

"Scripture and tradition form the core content of all adult catechesis...[u]se of Scripture and the Catechism...will help adults grasp the content of the faith and its practical application in Christian living."

(*OHWB*, USCCB, 88)

Why Catholic? is an easy-to-use tool for faith-sharing communities and individuals that focuses on the rich resources of the *Catechism of the Catholic Church*.This section highlights in detail the framework of the *Why Catholic?* process for each of the four books.

THE PROFESSION OF FAITH: WHAT WE BELIEVE BOOK 1

SCHEMA

"[I]t is intrinsic to faith that a believer desires to know better the One in whom he has put his faith and to understand better what He has revealed..." (CCC 158).

The first book in the *Why Catholic?* Series, *The Profession of Faith: What We Believe*, looks at the truths that we, as Catholics, believe and explores these basic tenets of our faith. It offers insights on what it means to be a Catholic, following "the oldest Roman catechism, the Apostles' Creed."

Session 1	Desire for God
Session 2	God's Revelation: Tradition and Scripture
Session 3	Faith: I Believe, We Believe
Session 4	The Trinity
Session 5	The Mystery of Creation
Session 6	The Incarnation
Session 7	The Public Life of Jesus
Session 8	The Paschal Mystery: Jesus' Death and Resurrection
Session 9	The Holy Spirit and the Church
Session 10	One Church with Diverse Roles

Session 11 Mary, Mother of Christ, Mother of the Church

Session 12 We Believe in Life Everlasting

ADULT FAITH FORMATION

In the U.S. Bishop's letter, *Our Hearts Were Burning Within Us: A Pastoral Plan for Adult Faith Formation in the United States*, the document states

- ❐ In light of the "unique opportunities and challenges..." our Church faces today, "adult faith formation must become our chief catechetical priority" (25).
- ❐ "Small communities are powerful vehicles for adult faith formation, providing opportunities for...the shared experience of Christian living and service to Church and society" (106).
- ❐ The leader is also a co-learner. The Emmaus story "offers us a model for our ministry and shows the need we all have for ongoing formation in faith" (12).
- ❐ The catechist of adults is a guide to learners as they seek to deepen their faith (149).

In the introduction of the document, *Our Hearts Were Burning Within Us*, the bishops speak of how the disciples of Jesus share in proclaiming the Good News to the entire world.

The *Why Catholic?* Series

- ❒ Makes this goal a reality
- ❒ Helps people take greater personal ownership of their faith
- ❒ Helps them move from inherited faith to deep faith conviction

The *Why Catholic?* Series helps people uncover their own story and journey.

- ❒ What does it mean to be Catholic?
- ❒ What is unique about Catholic Christian identity?
- ❒ Why do they remain Catholic?

OVERVIEW OF THE PROFESSION OF FAITH: WHAT WE BELIEVE

Part One of the *Catechism* focuses on The Profession of Faith, what we believe. It is structured around the Apostles' Creed. The Apostles' Creed states the central beliefs of our faith.

WHAT IS A CREED?

A creed is simply a statement of faith. When asked by Jesus Christ, "But who do you say that I am?" Peter's response was his creed: "You are the Messiah, the Son of the Living God" (Matthew 16:15-16). The English word "creed" comes from "credo" which means "I believe." Most creeds arose out of a need to address with the truth a particular heresy circulating at the time. Thus, each creed tends to place an emphasis on the principle of faith under attack at that time.

SESSION 1: DESIRE FOR GOD

Scripture: Luke 12:32-34. The heart's treasure. "For where your treasure is, there your heart will be also" (v. 34).

We begin with our desire for God. That desire for God is written in our hearts **(27)**. Within each person is a deep yearning for the holy. God also deeply desires our hearts and our love.

Session highlights

- ❒ Desire for God is written in the human heart.
- ❒ Ways of coming to know God
    1. The world's order and beauty
    2. The human person: soul and openness to truth and beauty
- ❒ How we speak about God

SESSION 2: GOD'S REVELATION: TRADITION AND SCRIPTURE

Scripture: 2 Peter 1:12-21. Keep your attention fixed on the message.

Our search for God requires every effort of intellect, a sound will, an upright heart as well as the witness of others who teach us to seek God. We can look to the physical world—the message of creation and the human person, the voice of conscience and arrive at certainty of the existence of God. We also know God's revelation through Tradition and Scripture **(82)**.

Session highlights

- ❒ Teachings of Jesus handed down through Sacred Tradition and Sacred Scripture
- ❒ Sacred Tradition - how it comes about
- ❒ Sacred Scripture - language, culture, events of the time
- ❒ Three criteria for interpreting Scripture

SESSION 3: FAITH: I BELIEVE, WE BELIEVE

Scripture: Hebrews 11:1-12. Recalls the faith of biblical figures.

The underlying question for us is do we believe? God constantly invites us into a grace-filled life of love and goodness. We have a choice. By faith we can respond, "Yes, Lord, I offer myself to you, do with me as you wish." It is the Holy Spirit that enables us to believe **(154)**. What is it that we believe? The basic truths of our faith are contained in the Apostles' Creed and the Nicene Creed.

Session highlights

- ❒ Faith: The first theological virtue
  1. Free gift—**Faith is an entirely free gift that God makes... (162).**
  2. Certain—**Faith...is more certain than all human knowledge because it is founded**

on the very word of God who cannot lie (157).

3. Freely given, faith must freely be received—**To be human...response to God by faith must be free...nobody is to be forced to embrace the faith against his will (160).**
4. Personal response—**...the free response of the human person to the initiative of God who reveals himself.... Our love for Jesus and for our neighbor impels us to speak to others about our faith (166).**

SESSION 4: THE TRINITY

Scripture: John 14:9-21, 25-26. "Whoever has seen me has seen the Father" (v. 9a).

The mystery of the Most Holy Trinity is the central mystery of Christian faith.... It is the mystery of God... (234). The mystery of love, "Whoever has seen me has seen the Father" (John 14:9a). The Holy Spirit will instruct you (John 14:26).

Session highlights

❒ Role of Father, Son, and Holy Spirit

❒ Our participation in the life of the Holy Trinity

SESSION 5: THE MYSTERY OF CREATION

Scripture: Genesis 1—2:4. Story of creation.

The New Testament reveals that God created everything by the eternal Word, his beloved Son

(John 1:1-3). **The Church's faith likewise confesses the creative action of the Holy Spirit... (291).** All three persons of the Blessed Trinity are involved in creation **(292)**.

Session highlights

❒ Suffering and evil in the world

❒ The role of the cross in understanding suffering

SESSION 6: THE INCARNATION

Scripture: John 1:1-5, 14. Prologue of John's Gospel.

Belief in the true Incarnation of the Son of God is the distinctive sign of Christian faith... (463). Throughout his public life, [Jesus] demonstrated his divine sovereignty by works of power over nature, illnesses, demons, death, and sin (447).

Session highlights

❒ Incarnation: the mystery of the union of the divine and human natures in the one person of the Word

SESSION 7: THE PUBLIC LIFE OF JESUS

Scripture: Luke 4:14-21. In the synagogue Jesus proclaims his mission.

Jesus' public life begins with his baptism by John... (535). His character and teachings were so attractive that people were constantly following him. A key theme in both the life and teaching of Jesus is the concept of the reign or the kingdom of God.

Session highlights

❒ Kingdom of God

❒ Parables
❒ Miracles

SESSION 8: THE PASCHAL MYSTERY: JESUS' DEATH AND RESURRECTION

Scripture: Mark 8:27-38. Peter declares Jesus as Messiah and the doctrine of the cross.

The cross is the unique sacrifice of Christ... (618) yet we, too, participate in it since Jesus united himself to all of us. **The truth of Jesus' divinity is confirmed by his Resurrection (653). ...Christ's Resurrection...is the principle and source of our future resurrection... (655).**

Session highlights

❒ Paschal Mystery has two aspects:

1. By his death, Christ liberates us from sin.
2. By his Resurrection, he opens for us the way to a new life.

SESSION 9: THE HOLY SPIRIT AND THE CHURCH

Scripture: 1 Corinthians 2:6-16. God reveals wisdom to us through the Spirit.

"Holy Spirit" is the proper name of the third person of the Trinity, the one whom we adore and glorify with God the Father and God the Son **(691). The mission of Christ and the Holy Spirit is brought to completion in the Church, which is the Body of Christ...**

(737). [The seven sacraments] **are actions of the Holy Spirit at work in...the Church... (1116).**

Session highlights

- ❒ Christ was filled with the Holy Spirit.
- ❒ The Holy Spirit continues to lead the Church.
- ❒ Sacraments are actions of the Holy Spirit.

SESSION 10: ONE CHURCH WITH DIVERSE ROLES

Scripture: John 17:1-26. Jesus' prayer to his Father for his disciples and all believers.

There are four characteristics of the Church and her mission: one, holy, catholic, and apostolic. **The Church is one *because of her "soul"*: "It is the Holy Spirit, dwelling in those who believe...brings about that wonderful communion of the faithful and joins them together**..." in unity (*Unitatis redintegratio* 2 § 2) **(813).** Holy Church is the holy people of God because God created her and the Spirit of holiness gives her life **(867). Catholic means "universal" ... or "in keeping with the whole" (830). The Church is apostolic because she is founded on the apostles... (857).**

Session highlights

- ❒ Church is one, holy, catholic, apostolic.
- ❒ While all are called to fulfill Christ's mission, we have different roles, for example, pope, bishops, priests, laity, members of religious communities.

SESSION 11: MARY, MOTHER OF CHRIST, MOTHER OF THE CHURCH

Scripture: Luke 1:26-56. Annunciation, Visitation, Magnificat.

We believe in **the communion of saints (946).** Those who have gone before us and have lived holy lives are very much alive to us today, and we are able to be in communion with them. Because Mary is the mother of Jesus who is the Son of God, Mary is the Mother of God **(963)**. [Mary's] **role in relation to the Church and to all humanity goes still further (968)**. We recognize her today as the **Mother of the Church (963)**.

Session highlights

❒ Mary: Mother of God, Mother of the Church, First Disciple

SESSION 12: WE BELIEVE IN LIFE EVERLASTING

Scripture: John 6:39-40. End of discourse on the Bread of Life. "I will raise them up."

This perfect life with the Most Holy Trinity...is called "heaven" (1024). By his death and Resurrection, Jesus Christ has "opened" heaven to us (1026). But **[t]o rise with Christ, we must die with Christ (1005). This state of definitive self-exclusion from communion with God and the blessed is called "hell" (1033).** The Church teaches that for those who still need to achieve such holiness after death there is a final purification—purgatory—that is entirely different from that of hell **(1030-1031)**.

Session highlights

- ❒ Heaven
- ❒ Hell
- ❒ Purgatory

THE CELEBRATION OF THE CHRISTIAN MYSTERY: SACRAMENTS BOOK 2

SCHEMA

"The fruit of sacramental life is both personal and ecclesial. For every one of the faithful on the one hand, this fruit is life for God in Christ Jesus; for the Church, on the other, it is an increase in charity and in her mission of witness" (1134).

The first four sessions of *The Celebration of the Christian Mystery: Sacraments* focus on the liturgy and an understanding of the sacraments. Then follow two sessions on baptism, one on the sacrament itself, and another on the Rite of Christian Initiation of Adults. The latter offers reflections not only on the Rite, but on its meaning for us and our parishes. The last six sessions focus on the other sacraments.

Session	1	God Acts through the Liturgy
Session	2	The Liturgy, the Work of God
Session	3	Celebrating the Liturgy
Session	4	God Acts through the Sacraments
Session	5	Baptism, a Sacrament of Initiation
Session	6	The Rite of Christian Initiation of Adults (RCIA)
Session	7	Confirmation, a Sacrament of Initiation

Session 8	Eucharist, a Sacrament of Initiation
Session 9	Penance and Reconciliation, a Sacrament of Healing
Session 10	The Anointing of the Sick, a Sacrament of Healing
Session 11	Holy Orders, a Sacrament at the Service of Communion
Session 12	Matrimony, a Sacrament at the Service of Communion

ADULT FAITH FORMATION

Our Hearts Were Burning Within Us, Part II, speaks of a mature Catholic faith as **living, explicit,** and **fruitful.** In essence the document explains each of these terms simply.

- ❐ A **living** faith means it is personal, a part of my daily life.
- ❐ An **explicit** faith means I understand it.
- ❐ A **fruitful** faith implies that my faith overflows in compassion, justice, and evangelization.

Why Catholic? fosters and promotes a mature Catholic faith.

- ❐ **Living:** The faith-sharing sessions give us the opportunity to pray about, reflect on, and share our faith. As we do, faith becomes more personal. We integrate it into our lives. Faith comes **alive.**

- ❒ **Explicit:** *Why Catholic?* encourages us to study our faith, read more about it in the *Catechism*, listen to others, and talk about it in a small group setting. As we do this, understanding grows. Faith becomes **explicit.**
- ❒ **Fruitful:** "Living the Good News" is an integral part of every faith-sharing session of *Why Catholic?* At each meeting, we are encouraged to decide upon an action response in order to live the Good News more intentionally. As we choose and fulfill our action responses, faith overflows in compassion, justice, and evangelization. Faith becomes **fruitful.**

OVERVIEW OF THE CELEBRATION OF THE CHRISTIAN MYSTERY: SACRAMENTS

SESSION I: GOD ACTS THROUGH THE LITURGY

Scripture: Luke 22:14-20. Consecration of bread and wine, Paschal Mystery.

We look at the reality that liturgy celebrates, namely, the Paschal Mystery of Jesus, his life, death and Resurrection. Liturgy means **"participation of the People of God in 'the work of God'"** (see John 17:4) **(1069).**

Session highlights

- ❐ Importance of liturgy in our lives
- ❐ Understanding of the Paschal Mystery
- ❐ How to prepare ourselves for liturgy

SESSION 2: THE LITURGY, THE WORK OF GOD (MASS)

Scripture: Ephesians 1:3-6. Christ brings us spiritual blessings.

In the eucharistic liturgy we celebrate the Paschal Mystery (life, death, and Resurrection) of Jesus (1085).

Session highlights

- ❐ Eucharistic liturgy, another term for the Mass
- ❐ Four ways Christ is present in the eucharistic liturgy
- ❐ Role of the Holy Spirit: sanctifying, understanding, union
- ❐ Liturgy of the Word and Eucharist

SESSION 3: CELEBRATING THE LITURGY

Scripture: Acts 2:42-47. Life among the followers: learning, liturgy, praying, sharing resources.

This session speaks of the richness of the word liturgy.

Session highlights

- ❐ Who celebrates liturgy? Action of the whole Church but there are different ministries
- ❐ How do we celebrate liturgy? Signs and symbols: light, darkness, candles, washing, anointing, bread, wine, Liturgy of the Word, music

- ❒ When do we celebrate liturgy? Sunday Mass. Easter—feast of feasts. At reception of sacraments, divine office
- ❒ Where is liturgy celebrated? Church

SESSION 4: GOD ACTS THROUGH THE SACRAMENTS (WHAT IS COMMON TO ALL SEVEN SACRAMENTS)

Scripture: Titus 2:11-14. God gave himself to rescue us from all that is evil. Live decent, honest lives, full of hope.

Session highlights

- ❒ Why sacraments are important
- ❒ How sacraments parallel life
- ❒ Grace
- ❒ Sacramental character or "seal"
- ❒ Sacraments are not magic
- ❒ Communal dimension of the sacraments

SESSION 5: BAPTISM, A SACRAMENT OF INITIATION

Scripture: Mark 1:1-11. The person and the preaching of John the Baptist. The baptism of Jesus.

Baptism, confirmation, and Eucharist are the three sacraments of initiation and **lay the foundations of every Christian life (1212).** Confirmation and Eucharist are intrinsically connected to baptism. We are strengthened in confirmation and we receive the food of eternal life in the Eucharist **(1212)**.

Session highlights

- ❒ Sacraments of Initiation lay the foundation of Christian life.
- ❒ Baptism
- ❒ Origin of the word: from the Greek, baptize, to immerse
    1. What happens at baptism?
    2. A new creature
    3. Freed from original sin
    4. Shares in the hope of resurrection
    5. Member of the Body of Christ (community among all Christians)
    6. Renewed by the Holy Spirit
    7. Begins ongoing conversion process
- ❒ Ongoing conversion process
    1. Post-baptismal catechumenate
    2. Grace of baptism
    3. Community helps us

SESSION 6: THE RITE OF CHRISTIAN INITIATION OF ADULTS (RCIA)

Scripture: Romans 6:3-11. Dead to sin but alive in Christ. All who share in the baptism of Christ share in his death and Resurrection.

Session highlights

- ❒ RCIA: Rite of Christian Initiation of Adults

- ❒ Catechumenate - the formation of persons who are preparing for baptism in preparation for their Christian Initiation **(1248)**.
- ❒ Stages of the RCIA: pre-catechumenate, catechumenate, purification and enlightenment, mystagogia.
- ❒ Rites of the RCIA: rite of acceptance, enrollment

SESSION 7: CONFIRMATION, A SACRAMENT OF INITIATION

Scripture: John 16:4-16. The work of the Holy Spirit. The promise of the Spirit.

Session highlights

- ❒ Jesus and the Holy Spirit
  1. Conceived by the Holy Spirit
  2. Guided and enlightened by the Holy Spirit
- ❒ Jesus promised the Holy Spirit
- ❒ Symbols of the Sacrament: oil, word, laying on hands
- ❒ Effects of confirmation
  1. Outpouring of the Holy Spirit
  2. Greater awareness of God with us and within us
  3. More closely united with Jesus and mission
  4. Recognize gifts of the Holy Spirit
  5. Empowered to go forth

SESSION 8: EUCHARIST, A SACRAMENT OF INITIATION

Scripture: John 6:48-58. "I am the bread of life." This is the bread that gives life. "...the one who eats this bread will live forever."

Session highlights

- ❒ Many names for Eucharist
- ❒ Two parts of the Mass
- ❒ Eucharist is sacrifice
- ❒ Heart of Eucharist is real presence
- ❒ Effects of receiving Eucharist
    1. Deeper union with Christ
    2. Share life of Christ
    3. We become the Church, the presence of Jesus in the world
    4. Commitment to the poor

SESSION 9: PENANCE AND RECONCILIATION, A SACRAMENT OF HEALING

Scripture: Luke 15:11-24. The Prodigal Son.

Session highlights

- ❒ Various names for the sacrament: penance, reconciliation, confession, etc.
- ❒ Forms of conversion: fasting, prayer, almsgiving
- ❒ Social dimension of sin
- ❒ How to go to confession

SESSION 10: THE ANOINTING OF THE SICK, A SACRAMENT OF HEALING

Scripture: James 5:14-16. Prayers of the community and the anointing of the sick.

Session highlights

- ❒ Meaning of suffering
- ❒ Progression of sacrament - extreme unction to anointing of the sick
- ❒ Communal aspect
- ❒ How it is celebrated
- ❒ Effects of the sacrament
  1. healing
  2. peace
  3. strength

SESSION 11: HOLY ORDERS, A SACRAMENT AT THE SERVICE OF COMMUNION

Scripture: Hebrews 5:1-10. Jesus is the great High Priest. God chooses Melchizedek.

Session highlights

- ❒ Two ways to participate in priesthood
  1. Common priesthood of all
  2. Ministerial priesthood
- ❒ Priesthood is about service
- ❒ Three groups who receive the sacrament of Holy Orders
- ❒ How the sacrament is conferred

SESSION 12: MATRIMONY, A SACRAMENT AT THE SERVICE OF COMMUNION

Scripture: 1 John 4:7-21. God is love. If we keep on loving others, we will stay one in our hearts with God, and he will stay one with us (unity). Marriage is centered in God **(1604)**.

Session highlights

- ❒ Marriage in the Old and New Testament
- ❒ How the sacrament is celebrated
- ❒ Purpose of marriage (holiness and children)
- ❒ Effects of the sacrament
- ❒ Annulments
- ❒ What sexuality is about
- ❒ The term, Domestic Church, indicates the family

LIFE IN CHRIST: WALKING WITH GOD BOOK 3

SCHEMA

"The human person participates in the light and power of the divine Spirit.... By free will, he is capable of directing himself toward his true good. He finds his perfection 'in seeking and loving what is true and good'" (1704).

The first six sessions of *Life in Christ: Walking with God* center on our freedom and responsibility, conscience, virtues, moral law, and grace. The second six sessions concentrate on the implications of the Ten Commandments.

Session	1	The Beatitudes
Session	2	Freedom and Responsibility of Human Acts
Session	3	Conscience
Session	4	Virtues
Session	5	Sin, Mercy, and Moral Solidarity
Session	6	Moral Law, Grace, and the Church
Session	7	Love of God
Session	8	Family
Session	9	Safeguarding Life and Truth
Session	10	Chastity and Love
Session	11	On Earthly Goods, Love for the Poor, and Work
Session	12	Human Fulfillment in Christ

ADULT FAITH FORMATION

THREE GOALS OF ADULT CATECHESIS IN THE CHRISTIAN COMMUNITY

(Summarized and adapted from *Our Hearts Were Burning Within Us,* pp. 22-24)

1. Invite and Enable Ongoing Conversion to Jesus in Holiness of Life

Our faith and life as adult disciples are grounded in developing a personal relationship with Jesus. At the heart of catechesis is the person of Jesus of Nazareth.

Catechesis aims at putting people in communion with Jesus Christ. Faith formation helps adults acquire an attitude of conversion to the Lord. It leads them to recognize and repent of sin, to seek reconciliation through the sacraments, to embrace the invitation and challenge of an ever-deepening faith in Jesus. It means putting on the mind of Christ, trusting in the Father's love, obeying God's will, seeking holiness of life, and growing in love for others.

Deepening personal prayer is a significant means toward growth in holiness.

2. Promote and Support Active Membership in the Christian Community

As adult believers, we learn and live our faith as active members of the Church. Our response to God's call to community "reveals itself concretely by a visible entry into a community of believers." People find this community of faith in the parish and diocese, in their families, small church communities, personal relationships, faith-based associations, and in the communion of saints of all times and places. [F]aith formation helps adults make "a conscious and firm decision to live the gift and choice of faith through membership in the Christian community...coresponsibility for the community's mission and internal life." They contribute to its life and mission through the generous stewardship of their gifts.

3. Call and Prepare Adults to Act as Disciples in Mission to the World

The Church and its adult faithful have a mission to share the message of Christ to renew and to transform the social and temporal order. This dual calling to evangelization and justice is integral to the identity of the lay faithful; all are called to it in baptism. [F]aith formation seeks to help each adult believer become "more willing and able to be a Christian disciple in the world." [A]dult disciples give witness to God's love so, in the power of the Spirit, they renew the face of the earth.

OVERVIEW OF LIFE IN CHRIST: WALKING WITH GOD

SESSION 1: THE BEATITUDES

Scripture: Matthew 5:3-12. Beatitudes. We believe that God has a purpose for each of us and we want to do God's will in our lives.

Session highlights

- ❐ Called to be disciples, we are given the Holy Spirit and intellectual power of reasoning to follow the example of Christ.
- ❐ Beatitudes are blueprints for living the Christian life.

SESSION 2: FREEDOM AND RESPONSIBILITY OF HUMAN ACTS

Scripture: John 13:31-45; 14:15-17; 15:1-27. Exodus 19:3-6; 20:1-17. Love one another, sending of the Holy Spirit, vine and branches, Jesus calls us friends, faithfulness of God, Ten Commandments. The *Catechism* emphasizes the freedom and responsibility that God gives us **(1730)**.

Session highlights

- ❐ Given freedom to choose, we recognize actions have consequences
- ❐ How the morality of an action is determined
- ❐ God's rules for living are written in our hearts
- ❐ The natural law and the Ten Commandments are moral principles

Please note: There are many Scripture readings in this session.

SESSION 3: CONSCIENCE

Scripture: Romans 1:32; 2:14-16; 1 John 3:19-20. The demands of the law are written on our hearts **(1777-1778)**. Being committed to the truth and keeping the commandments.

Session highlights

- ❐ The importance of developing a good moral conscience
- ❐ How to develop a good moral conscience

SESSION 4: VIRTUES

Scripture: John 15:9-10; Matthew 22:36-40; 1 Corinthians 13:1-7. Abide in my love, great commandments, gift of love—"[love] bears all things" (1 Corinthians 13:7).

Session highlights

- ❐ Virtues
- ❐ Four moral virtues
- ❐ Three theological virtues
- ❐ Importance of the Holy Spirit

SESSION 5: SIN, MERCY, AND MORAL SOLIDARITY

Scripture: John 4:4-30. Samaritan Woman.

Session highlights

- ❐ Sin
- ❐ Mortal and venial sin
- ❐ Common good and what it presupposes
- ❐ Social justice
- ❐ Three aspects necessary for social justice

SESSION 6: MORAL LAW, GRACE, AND THE CHURCH

Scripture: Colossians 1:2b-6a. The gospel, the message of truth has taken root in your life.

Session highlights

- ❒ Moral law
- ❒ Natural law
- ❒ Grace
- ❒ Actual grace
- ❒ Sanctifying grace

SESSION 7: LOVE OF GOD

Scripture: Matthew 19:16-21. Rich man, sell your possessions.

Session highlights

- ❒ Ten Commandments
- ❒ First three Commandments - Love
- ❒ Importance of the Sabbath

SESSION 8: FAMILY

Scripture: Luke 2:41-52. Jesus in the Temple.

Session highlights

- ❒ Domestic Church - the family
- ❒ Role of parents and children

SESSION 9: SAFEGUARDING LIFE AND TRUTH

Scripture: Matthew 5:21-24; 39. Against anger, abusive language. Be reconciled before coming to the altar. Offer no resistance to injury.

Session highlights

- ❒ Fifth Commandment - Thou shall not kill: death penalty, abortion, euthanasia, war
- ❒ Eighth Commandment - Live the truth, lying and the truth, deception of the media

SESSION 10: CHASTITY AND LOVE

Scripture: John 15:9-17. A disciple's love. "I call you friends" (v. 15).

The session explores sexuality in great detail, the meaning of married love, and many moral challenges we face.

Session highlights

- ❒ Sixth Commandment - You shall not commit adultery.
- ❒ Ninth Commandment - You shall not covet your neighbor's wife or husband.

SESSION 11: ON EARTHLY GOODS, LOVE FOR THE POOR, AND WORK

Scripture: Luke 19:1-10. Zacchaeus.

Session highlights

- ❒ Seventh Commandment - You shall not steal. Stealing has to do with reputation, wages, respect for earth, property, and justice.

- ❒ Right to work
- ❒ Rights of the worker
- ❒ Value of work
- ❒ Commitment to the poor
- ❒ Responsibility of rich nations to poorer nations

Please note: This session covers many issues.

SESSION 12: HUMAN FULFILLMENT IN CHRIST

Scripture: Luke 21:1-4. Widow's Mite.

Session highlights

- ❒ Tenth Commandment - You shall not covet your neighbor's goods.
- ❒ Greed, avarice, envy

CHRISTIAN PRAYER: DEEPENING MY EXPERIENCE OF GOD BOOK 4

SCHEMA

"Christian prayer is a covenant relationship between God and man in Christ. It is the action of God and man, springing forth from both the Holy Spirit and ourselves, wholly directed to the Father, in union with the human will of the Son of God made man" (2564).

The first three sessions of *Christian Prayer: Deepening My Experience of God* focus on prayer itself and how God communicates with us. The next sessions look at different forms of prayer and some difficulties we experience in prayer. The last three sessions offer a deeper look at the prayer that Jesus taught us, the Lord's Prayer.

Session 1 What Is Prayer?
Session 2 Prayer in the Old Testament
Session 3 Jesus and Mary Teach Us to Pray
Session 4 Forms of Prayer
Session 5 The Sources and Way of Prayer
Session 6 Guides for Prayer
Session 7 Vocal Prayer and Meditation
Session 8 Contemplative Prayer

Session	9	Difficulties in Prayer
Session	10	The Lord's Prayer
Session	11	The Lord's Prayer (continued)
Session	12	The Lord's Prayer (continued)

ADULT FAITH FORMATION

Six Dimensions for Adult Faith Formation Content are found in *Our Hearts Were Burning Within Us* (pp. 28-33).

❐ Knowledge of the Faith

❐ Liturgical Life

❐ Moral Formation

❐ Prayer

❐ Communal Life

❐ Missionary Spirit

We can look at each of these individually and how they correspond with aspects of *Why Catholic?*

❐ Knowledge of the Faith

The entire content of *Why Catholic?* especially Book I, *The Profession of Faith: What We Believe*, gives us knowledge about the essentials of our faith. A deacon who used these materials said he had received his education in Catholic grade school, high school, college, and later was formed and educated to be a deacon. Yet, he was still learning new things about his faith through *Why Catholic?*

❒ **Liturgical Life**

The second book, *The Celebration of the Christian Mystery: Sacraments*, focuses on the liturgy and an understanding of the sacraments.

❒ **Moral Formation**

The third book, *Life in Christ: Walking with God*, focuses on our moral formation; formation of conscience, freedom, responsibility, virtues, moral law, and grace. Through a presentation of the Beatitudes and the Ten Commandments, moral formation is further explored.

❒ **Prayer**

While the entire *Why Catholic?* Series promotes and encourages Christian prayer, the fourth book of the series, *Christian Prayer: Deepening My Experience of God*, provides a variety of prayer experiences and explains the background of each. The pivotal Christian prayer, the Lord's Prayer, is the focus of three complete sessions.

❒ **Communal Life**

Throughout the four books, the communal life of the Church is stressed: 1) in what we believe, 2) in how we worship, 3) in how we relate to one another, and 4) in how we pray.

❒ **Missionary Spirit**

The "Living the Good News" section at the end of each session reminds participants they are to live out their faith in their personal lives, family lives, and in society. With concrete suggestions to stimulate and guide them, participants capture the missionary spirit of the Church in which we are initiated in baptism.

OVERVIEW OF CHRISTIAN PRAYER: DEEPENING MY EXPERIENCE OF GOD

Christian Prayer: Deepening My Experience of God unfolds for us the richness of our prayer life. The first few sessions focus on prayer itself and how God communicates with us. The next sessions look at different forms of prayer and some difficulties we may experience in prayer. The last sessions (10-12) offer a deeper look at the prayer that Jesus taught us, the Our Father.

- ❒ Sessions 5, 7, and 8 have prayer experiences within them.
- ❒ Session 5 - You will need a copy of the *Catechism* for your small community meeting for all to read paragraphs 2676 and 2677 for the prayer experience.
- ❒ The Lord's Prayer is covered in the last three sessions (10-12).

SESSION 1: WHAT IS PRAYER?

Scripture: Luke 18:9-14. Pharisee and tax collector.

Session highlights

❒ The meaning of prayer

❒ Where prayer comes from

SESSION 2: PRAYER IN THE OLD TESTAMENT

Scripture: Genesis 12:1-9; 15:1-6. Abram's call and migration. The covenant with Abram.

Session highlights

❒ Prayers of Abraham, Moses, Hannah, and Elijah

❒ Book of Psalms

❒ Contemplative and intercessory prayer

SESSION 3: JESUS AND MARY TEACH US TO PRAY

Scripture: Mark 1:32-35. After healing, Jesus goes off to pray.

Session highlights

❒ Jesus teaches us to pray

❒ Jesus calls us to conversion and faith

❒ Mary teaches us to pray

SESSION 4: FORMS OF PRAYER

Scripture: Ephesians 1:3-6. A prayer of praise speaking of God's plan of salvation.

Session highlights

❒ Prayers of blessing and adoration, petition, intercession, thanksgiving, and praise

SESSION 5: THE SOURCES AND WAY OF PRAYER

Scripture: Romans 5:1-4. Prayer of praise to God even for afflictions.

Session highlights

- ❒ How we learn to pray
- ❒ Styles of prayer

Prayer Experiences

- ❒ Close your eyes and concentrate on breathing. Breathe in the life of the Spirit, breathe out cares and worries. Repeat the name of Jesus (10 min.).
- ❒ Read a prayer slowly and reflectively.
- ❒ Read together from the *Catechism,* paragraphs 2676 and 2677; prayerfully reflect on the Hail Mary.

SESSION 6: GUIDES FOR PRAYER

Scripture: 1 Thessalonians 1:2-10. A prayer of gratitude for the faithful.

Session highlights

- ❒ Various spiritualities in the Church
- ❒ Who teaches us to pray?
- ❒ Where can we pray?
- ❒ Times for prayer

SESSION 7: VOCAL PRAYER AND MEDITATION

Scripture: John 4:4-30. Samaritan woman, (used during the group meditation.)

Session highlights

- ❒ Vocal prayer - speaking to God
- ❒ Meditation - listening to God

Prayer Experience

- ❒ 20 min. Group meditation on the Samaritan woman (20 min.)

SESSION 8: CONTEMPLATIVE PRAYER

Scripture: Song of Songs 2:8-17. Beautiful description of God's love for the beloved.

Session highlights

- ❒ Contemplative prayer—simply being present to God

Prayer Experience

- ❒ Contemplative prayer—gazing upon an icon or picture of Jesus (20 min.)

SESSION 9: DIFFICULTIES IN PRAYER

Scripture: Matthew 6:19-34. True riches—where does your heart lie? Prayer of humility, trust and perseverance.

Session highlights

- ❒ Difficulties in prayer
- ❒ How to overcome some of the obstacles

SESSION 10: THE LORD'S PRAYER

Scripture: Matthew 6:9-13. The Lord's Prayer.

Session highlights

- ❐ The Our Father provides us with the words to pray and a model for prayer.
- ❐ The Lord's Prayer is at the center of the Church's prayer.

SESSION 11: THE LORD'S PRAYER (CONTINUED)

Scripture: Matthew 5:21-26. How to be reconciled in the community.

Session highlights

- ❐ When we pray the Our Father:
    1. We offer prayers of adoration, love and blessing by saying "Our Father, who art in heaven."
    2. The next part contains seven petitions.
    3. The first three petitions strengthen us in faith, hope, and love.

SESSION 12: THE LORD'S PRAYER (CONTINUED)

Scripture: Luke 11:5-13. Be persistent in your prayer.

Session highlights

- ❐ Final four petitions remind us of our great need for God's help and grace.
- ❐ Our daily bread is physical, emotional, and spiritual.

FAITH AND LEADERSHIP FORMATION

As a small community leader, you will be facilitating the faith learning experience of those in your small group. RENEW International offers adult faith learning experiences to help you strengthen and deepen your faith and grow in Christian leadership skills. You are strongly encouraged to attend the Small Community Leader Workshops that will be offered to prepare you for leading the sessions in each book. We also invite you to attend the Faith Formation Workshops and Retreats to strengthen and expand your knowledge of the Catholic faith and to deepen your relationship with God and the Church. Please encourage each of the participants in your small community to attend the Faith Formation Workshops and the Retreats. Also invite and welcome others who may be interested. The Faith Formation Workshops and Retreats are a great way to encourage and inspire others to join a small group.

BOOK ONE—THE PROFESSION OF FAITH: WHAT WE BELIEVE

Small Community Leader Formation Workshop—The Profession of Faith: What We Believe

Focuses on our desire for God and the basic tenets of our faith as expressed in the Apostles' Creed, with special emphasis on the central mystery of our Christian faith—the Holy Trinity. Also offers practical skills to facilitate adult learning through the *Why Catholic?* program.

Target audience: small community leaders, *Why Catholic?* Team

Faith Formation Workshop—Scripture and Tradition: The Braid of Revelation

Centers around the Christian conviction that in Jesus Christ, God has fully revealed himself to humanity. Through the braiding together of Scripture and Tradition, the presence and meaning of Christ in the world is discovered.

Target audience: *Why Catholic?* Team, small community leaders, participants in small communities, catechists, RCIA candidates, total parish

Retreat Experience—Discovering God in the Ordinary

Provides an opportunity for reflecting on the infinite beauty of the Creator in creation. Explores the experience of encountering the God revealed in Jesus Christ in our everyday life. Participants are invited into silence, prayer, and ritual.

Target audience: *Why Catholic?* Team, small community leaders, participants in small communities, total parish

BOOK TWO—THE CELEBRATION OF THE CHRISTIAN MYSTERY: SACRAMENTS

Small Community Leader Formation Workshop—The Celebration of the Christian Mystery: Sacraments

Looks at the understanding of liturgy and the sacraments as doors to the sacred. Especially explores the sacrament of the Eucharist and its meaning in our lives.
Target audience: small community leaders, *Why Catholic?* Team

Faith Formation Workshop—The Body of Christ: Jesus' Presence in the Liturgy

Fosters growth, understanding, and appreciation of Christ as the sacrament of God's presence in the world. Emphasizes the real presence in the Eucharist and Catholics' participation in the Mass and other sacraments.
Target audience: *Why Catholic?* Team, small community leaders, participants in small communities, catechists, RCIA candidates, total parish

Retreat Experience—Eucharist: Bread for the Journey of Life

Reflects on how the love of God comes to us as sacramental presence, individually and as community, enabling perseverance on the journey of faith.
Target audience: *Why Catholic?* Team, small community leaders, participants in small communities, total parish

BOOK THREE—LIFE IN CHRIST: WALKING WITH GOD

Small Community Leader Formation Workshop—Life in Christ: Walking with God

Jesus models for us a new attitude based on right relationships and love. Explores both the Ten Commandments and the Beatitudes as sources of moral principle and blueprints for living the Christian life.
Target audience: small community leaders, *Why Catholic?* Team

Faith Formation Workshop—Living Gospel Values in the 21st Century

Explores biblical justice as a way of connecting faith to everyday life. Focuses on right relationships, and reviews Catholic social teaching. Participants practice the Observe, Judge, Act model of Christian decision-making.
Target audience: *Why Catholic?* Team, small community leaders, participants in small communities, catechists, RCIA candidates, total parish

Retreat Experience—Walking with Christ: Living the Beatitudes

Focuses on integrating the Word of God and the Church's teachings into our daily lives. Particular emphasis is placed on understanding the importance of quiet reflection time.

Target audience: *Why Catholic?* Team, small community leaders, participants in small communities, total parish community

BOOK FOUR—CHRISTIAN PRAYER: DEEPENING MY EXPERIENCE OF GOD

Small Community Leader Formation Workshop—Christian Prayer: Deepening My Experience of God

Addresses the types, forms, and expressions of prayer with special emphasis on the Our Father. A number of prayer forms are experienced. Leaders are assisted in learning various ways to enhance prayer in their small communities.

Target audience: small community leaders, *Why Catholic?* Team

Faith Formation Workshop—Prayer: Many Methods, One Purpose

Looks at the richness of prayer in our Catholic heritage. Provides an opportunity for participants to grow in their awareness, understanding, and appreciation of prayer forms of meditation and contemplation as helpful and meaningful ways of praying; explores the challenges of listening and praying even in periods of dryness.

Target audience: *Why Catholic?* Team, small community leaders, participants in small communities, catechists, RCIA candidates, total parish

Retreat Experience—Sitting by the Well: Meeting Jesus in Prayer

Engages participants in an experience of reflecting on the gospel passage of the Samaritan Woman, using imagination, heart, mind, and action.

Target audience: *Why Catholic?* Team, small community leaders, participants in small communities, total parish

RESOURCES

Our Hearts Were Burning Within Us: A Pastoral Plan for Adult Faith Formation in the United States. Washington, DC: USCCB, 1999.

Libreria Editrice Vaticana. *Catechism of the Catholic Church.* Washington, DC: United States Catholic Conference, 1994. English translation of the *Catechism of the Catholic Church* for the United States of America Copyright © 1994, United States Conference of Catholic Bishops. English translation of the *Catechism of the Catholic Church: Modifications from the Editio Typica* Copyright ©1997, United States Conference of Catholic Bishops.

RESOURCES AVAILABLE FROM RENEW INTERNATIONAL

Small Christian Communities: A Vision of Hope for the 21st Century Revised and Expanded. Mahwah, NJ: Paulist Press, 2003.

The People's Prayer Book: Personal and Group Prayers. Liguori, MO: Liguori Publications, 2003.

Great Ideas from Great Parishes: A Parish Handbook. Liguori, MO: Liguori Publications, 2003.

Small Community Leader Training Video. Plainfield, NJ: RENEW International.

RENEW International

1232 George Street

Plainfield, NJ 07062-1717

Web sites	www.renewintl.org
	www.whycatholic.org
E-mail	Resources@renewintl.org
Toll free	888-433-3221
Questions	908-769-5400